Kiddles

I0171879

Riddles for Kids

Cloud Kingdom Games

Contributors & Editors:

   Doug Carr
   Esther Carr
   Robin Marks
   Steve Martin
   Matt Mayfield
   Vicky Mayfield
   Rick Smith
   Rod Stephens

Cover art:

   Amber Mayfield

ISBN 978-1-928807-17-9
Shelve under Games & Puzzles

What are Kiddles?

Kiddles are riddles for kids!

These riddles are rhyming poems that ask the question "what am I?"

On the page across from each riddle is a picture showing many things. Somewhere hidden in that picture is the answer to the riddle. If you think you've figured out the answer, take a look at the picture page. If you see your answer, you are probably right! If you don't see your answer, you should try to solve the riddle again.

The answers to each riddle are printed upside down on the next page.

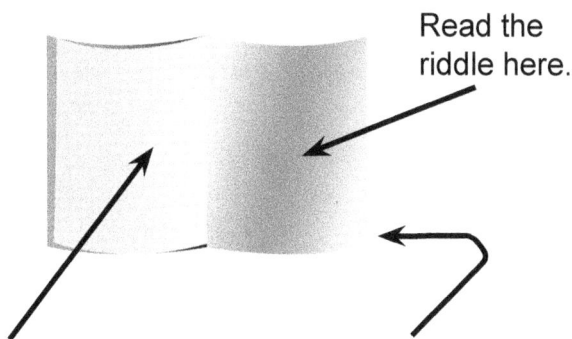

Read the riddle here.

Look in the picture here for a hint.

The answer is written upside down on the bottom of the next page.

If you're stumped or just not sure what some of the lines in the riddle mean then turn to the riddle explanations starting on page 74. Make sure you have already tried to answer the riddle before looking here, because the explanations often have the answer in them.

We've also hidden the words to a riddle somewhere in the book, can you find it?

Ready to start? Turn the page and let the kiddling begin!

A Bunch

A bunch of circles on some squares.

Half like fire,

Half like night.

When each of them becomes a king,

Now twice as big

Keep up the fight.

What is it?

Look at this page for a hint

Look on the next page for the answer

A comet

It flies just like a comet

And rolls across the land

Chased by those who follow

And touch it with no hands

With feet and heads they move it

As cheers come from the stands.

What is it?

Look at this page for a hint

Look on the next page for the answer

Answer to A **Comet:** Soccer Ball

He Doesn't Eat

He doesn't eat,
yet he gets full.

He's very old,
but sometimes new.

The highest hurdle
for a cow.

This man looks down
on me and you.

What is it?

Look at this page for a hint

Look on the next page for the answer

The Emperor

An emperor
without a crown.

Always wears
his formal gown.

He falls in water
and doesn't drown.

Atop a globe
that's upside-down.

What is it?

Look at this page for a hint

Look on the next page for the answer

Yellow

A Horseshoe

Like a horseshoe hanging
with its points down

Whenever you are sad.

To turn this horseshoe
right-side up,

Simply become glad.

What is it?

Look at this page for a hint ⟵   Look on the next page for the answer ⟶

Marshmallows

Like marshmallows tumbling
from the sky,

When all the leaves have
changed and died.

On top of it kids like to fly.

This blanket isn't warm.

Angels wave their arms around,

Men are made all over town,

Tickles your nose and
cures your frown.

Left over from a storm.

What is it?

Look at this page for a hint   Look on the next page for the answer

Mountains

I saw a pair of mountains,

I saw them walk away,

I saw them carry water,

Where water's far away.

In a burning, shifting land,

They slowly walked
across the sand.

What is it?

Look at this page for a hint ← | → Look on the next page for the answer

A

A net on the Breeze

I cast my net upon the breeze

To catch the fishes of the sky.

I catch them with the
greatest ease,

Although myself I cannot fly.

I watch and wait so patiently,

With my many legs and eyes.

What is it?

Look at this page for a hint

Look on the next page for the answer

Singer's

Answer to **A Net On the Breeze:** Spider

NiGht MOuse

I'm a mouse in the night,

I eat in my flight,

I like to sleep,

Below my feet,

Watch out that I don't bite!

What is it?

Look at this page for a hint

Look on the next page for the answer

Answer to **NiGht MOUSe**: Bat

NO nose?

No nose to smell,

No hands to hold,

Never hears a sound.

Never sees with its eyes

Buried under ground.

Great grated,

A smash mashed,

Fries from France are found.

What is it?

Look at this page for a hint ⟵

Look on the next page for the answer ⟶

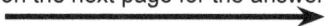

Answer to **NO NOSE?**: Potato

Simple Journey

This simple journey will begin

When you get just one foot in

Left or right, always around

Shake it up and you'll have found...

The meaning of it all.

What Dance is it?

Look at this page for a hint ←

Look on the next page for the answer →

Answer to *Simple Journey*: Dancing the Hokey Pokey

Sometimes Soft

Sometimes soft as rubber.

Sometimes hard as brick.

Binds things tight together;

Trucks will mix it thick.

What is it?

Look at this page for a hint   Look on the next page for the answer

Answer to **Sometimes Soft:** Cement

Not a Man

Not a man,

And not a mouse,

Though both can
frighten me.

Big as a house,

Don't pack my trunk

Or play my ivory.

What is it?

Look at this page for a hint

Look on the next page for the answer

you

SinG a Pretty SonG

This bird won't sit out
in your tree

And sing a pretty song.

Instead it makes a
great big roar

And takes a journey long.

Although its wings
themselves won't flap.

It can carry you along.

What is it?

Look at this page for a hint

Look on the next page for the answer

FIND

Answer to Sing a Pretty Song: Airplane

White Flesh

White flesh,

Drinks dew,

Gives milk, won't moo.

Hairy head, over sands,

Think of palms,

Not of hands.

What is it?

Look at this page for a hint ⟵   Look on the next page for the answer ⟶

Across the Plain

With a bound it
roams around

Across the distant plain.

With a roar
it roams some more

And shakes its mighty
mane.

What is it?

Look at this page for a hint ←

Look on the next page for the answer →

In

Green Raft

A raft of green that stays afloat,

But not a raft, and not a boat.

A disc with anchor down below,

An anchor from which it did grow.

Perhaps in marsh, pond or bog

Or bogged down by a weary frog.

What is it?

Look at this page for a hint

Look on the next page for the answer

Answer to **Green Raft:** Lily Pad

After Rain

After rain.

On a box.

In the hair.

With a fiddle.

What is it?

Look at this page for a hint ⟵

Look on the next page for the answer ⟶

Answer to *After Rain*: Bow

Goes Around

What goes around comes around

Or so they say.

Thrown for a loop

In down under play.

What is it?

Look at this page for a hint ←

Look on the next page for the answer →

BOOK

I Sleep

I sleep by day and fly by night.

The moon hides me from peoples' sight.

Reach for me but always fail.

Trust in me when you set sail.

What is it?

Look at this page for a hint

Look on the next page for the answer

KEPT

Answer to | **Sleep**: Star

Sometimes Inside

Sometimes inside,

Sometimes outside,

Sometimes it's not there at all.

Life needs form and structure,

Without me you would fall.

What is it?

Look at this page for a hint

Look on the next page for the answer

AND

Answer to **Sometimes Inside**: Skeleton

Hunter

The hunter far and wide will roam,

Like a ghost of sun and shadow.

First she'll brush then find the comb,

And then put on a dancing show.

Mother waits inside her home,

Where golden treasure flows.

What is it?

Look at this page for a hint
Look on the next page for the answer

Answer to **Hunter:** Bee

Home

A home made out of water

A home as hard as steel

Where nighttime can be brilliant

And daytime darkness real.

What is it?

Look at this page for a hint

Look on the next page for the answer

Answer to **HOME**: Igloo

Drowsy

Beneath the drowsy summer sun

I spread my golden hair.

From dawn until the day is done

I lie without a care.

My locks soon turn from gold to white,

As they get set to flee.

My hair comes loose and takes to flight

Adrift upon the breeze.

What is it?

Look at this page for a hint

Look on the next page for the answer

Answer to **prowsy**: Dandelion

Downside

With downside dark

And upside pale

You run from me

When I turn tail.

What is it?

Look at this page for a hint

Look on the next page for the answer

Behind

One behind, and one
between,

One stands on a hill.

Three on three, and three
around,

A test of strength and skill.

What is it?

Look at this page for a hint

Look on the next page for the answer

Answer to **Behind**: Baseball

TWO Arms

Two arms, no hands

Four legs, no feet

One back, no spine

No lap, one seat.

What is it?

Look at this page for a hint

Look on the next page for the answer

YOU'RE

Answer to **TWO ARMS**: Chair

TWO MORE ARMS

Two short arms and head
like a rock

Hanging around on a city
block;

Wrench my arms, and you'll
get wet,

But I'll get water from your
pet.

What is it?

Look at this page for a hint
Look on the next page for the answer

Surprised

Answer to **TWO MORE ARMS:** Fire hydrant

Ballet

I'm found in the ballet.

I'm a dance or a room.

I'm also hidden in

A helium balloon.

If you're having fun,

You might have one of me.

Hard and soft and basket,

Foot and base and tee.

What is it?

Look at this page for a hint ⟵

Look on the next page for the answer ⟶

Answer to **Ballet**: Ball

BLACK AND WHITE

A killer clad in black and white.

Big, not sad, when blue.

Great and white inspired spite,

And gray's the other hue.

What is it?

Look at this page for a hint ←   Look on the next page for the answer →

Answer to **Black and White**: Whale

Sleeps

It sleeps for years and suddenly wakes

It shifts in bed, its body shakes.

Its blood flows red then turns to black.

It sleeps again but may come back.

What is it?

Look at this page for a hint
←

Look on the next page for the answer
→

Weather

In any weather we can thrive --

We flow across the plain,

And since we never are alive

We never can be slain.

Our presence you might never lack --

We never leave for long.

You chop us down -- we grow right back

An army thousands strong.

What is it?

Look at this page for a hint

Look on the next page for the answer

Answer to **weather**: Hair

A Worker

A worker, tireless, straight and tall.

His own little room,

he leans against the wall.

His dirty hair, hanging down,

Dry and dusty on the ground.

Push him around as much as you can,

Towards the edge, the edge of a pan.

What is it?

Look at this page for a hint

Look on the next page for the answer

RIGHT

Water and Sun

Born of the mixture of water and sun,

A marvel of beauty if ever was one.

A cloak of majesty worn by the sky,

No one can touch it but all dreamers try.

What is it?

Here

Smiles

Always smiles or maybe frowns

Sinks in water, never drowns.

Catches prey on its barbed teeth

Hunts all day, but never eats.

What is it?

Look at this page for a hint

←

Look on the next page for the answer

→

Explanation

Was there something about one of the riddles that you didn't understand? Go ahead and look at the these pages - for each riddle we'll explain what the lines of the riddle mean. Don't look here first though, make sure you try to solve the riddle!

A Bunch
A bunch of circles on some squares.
Half like fire;
Half like night.
When each of them becomes a king,
Now twice as big keep up the fight.

The squares are the checker board. One player is red and the other is black. When your piece get's kinged it's twice as big.

A Comet
It flies just like a comet
And rolls across the land
Chased by those who follow
And touch it with no hands
With feet and heads they move it
As cheers come from the stands.

Comets are usually in space but these are on the ground. Each team tries to keep it away from the other team. Only the goal keeper can touch it with their hands during play. Go team!

He Doesn't Eat

He doesn't eat,
yet he gets full.
He's very old,
but sometimes new.
The highest hurdle
for a cow.
This man looks down
on me and you.

Sometimes the moon is full and sometimes it's new. The cow jumped over it and then the dish ran away with the spoon. Hello man in the moon! How are you?

The Emperor

An emperor
without a crown.
Always wears
his formal gown.
He falls in water
and doesn't drown.
Atop a globe
that's upside-down.

The Emperor penguin is a kind of penguin, the largest in fact. It looks like he's wearing a tuxedo. He doesn't drown because he can swim (very quickly, too). He's found in Antarctica which is at the bottom of the globe.

A Horseshoe

Like a horseshoe hanging with its points down
Whenever you are sad.

To turn this horseshoe
right-side up,
Simply become glad.

Think of what a horseshoe looks like when it's turned upside down. Now look at yourself in the mirror when you're sad. Be happy then you can smile!

Explanations

75

Marshmallows
Like marshmallows tumbling
from the sky,
When all the leaves have
changed and died.
On top of it kids like to fly.
This blanket isn't warm.

Angels wave their arms around,
Men are made all over town,
Tickles your nose and
cures your frown.
Left over from a storm.

Imagine marshmallows falling in the fall and winter. Kids like to fly on sleds, skis or snow boards. A blanket of snow isn't as warm as a cloth one. Don't forget to build a snowman!

Mountains
I saw a pair of mountains,
I saw them walk away,
I saw them carry water,
Where water's far away.
In a burning, shifting land,
They slowly walked
across the sand.

A Bactrian camel has two humps that look sort of like mountains. They carry water, but not in the humps, the humps are actually full of fat. Although they can live elsewhere, they're best known for being in the desert.

A Net on the Breeze
I cast my net upon the breeze
To catch the fishes of the sky.
I catch them with the
greatest ease,
Although myself I cannot fly.

I watch and wait so patiently,
With my many legs and eyes.

*Spiders make webs to catch the "Fishes of the sky" - the bugs
they eat. Most of them have eight eyes and legs.*

Night Mouse
I'm a mouse in the night,
I eat in my flight,
I like to sleep,
Below my feet,
Watch out that I don't bite!

*A bat looks a lot like a mouse with wings. Many scoop up
insects as they fly, although some also eat just fruit. Most bats
will sleep upside down, hanging from their feet.*

No Nose
No nose to smell,
No hands to hold,
Never hears a sound.
Never sees with its eyes
Buried under ground.
Great grated, a smash mashed,
Fries from France are found.

*It has a stalk but no arms or legs. Its seeds are called "eyes".
There are lots of ways to eat them, too.*

Explanations

Simple Journey

This simple journey will begin
When you get just one foot in
Left or right, always around
Shake it up and you'll have found...
The meaning of it all.

You put your right foot in, you put your right foot out. You put your right foot in and you shake it all about. You do the hokey-pokey and you turn yourself around. That's what it's all about!

Sometimes Soft

Sometimes soft as rubber.
Sometimes hard as brick.
Binds things tight together;
Trucks will mix it thick.

Rubber cement is one kind. The kind they make sidewalks out of is another, which gets mixed in a cement truck.

Not a Man

Not a man,
And not a mouse,
Though both can
frighten me.

Big as a house,
Don't pack my trunk
Or play my ivory.

In stories, elephants are afraid of mice. Well, maybe they're not as big as all houses, but they're bigger than some. Their tusks are ivory which is what we call the white keys on a piano.

Sing a Pretty Song

This bird won't sit out in your tree
And sing a pretty song.
Instead it makes a great big roar
And takes a journey long.
Although its wings themselves won't flap.
It can carry you along.

The "bird" is the airplane. Jets, in particular, are very loud. The wings stay nice and steady while you sit inside and look down on the tops of the clouds.

White Flesh

White flesh, drinks dew,
Gives milk, won't moo.
Hairy head, over sands,
Think of palms, not of hands.

The inside of the coconut is white, the tree drinks water. You get coconut milk from them - not cow's milk. They grow on coconut palm trees.

Across the plain

With a bound it roams around
Across the distant plain
With a roar it roams some more
And shakes its mighty mane

They're strong and fast, most of them are in Africa except for the ones in zoos.

Green Raft

A raft of green that stays afloat,
But not a raft, and not a boat.
A disc with anchor down below,
An anchor from which it did grow.
Perhaps in marsh, pond or bog
Or bogged down by a weary frog.

They are disc shaped with a root that is at the bottom of the pond. At least in stories, frogs sit on them.

Explanations

After rain

After rain.
On a box.
In the hair.
With a fiddle.

After it rains you might see a rainbow. If it's a nicely wrapped present, it might have a bow on top. Little girls sometimes wear them in their hair. You'll need one to play the fiddle.

Goes Around

What goes around comes around
Or so they say.
Thrown for a loop
In down under play.

It returns when thrown - or at least it is supposed to. Australia is "down under" and that is the where boomerangs were invented.

I Sleep

I sleep by day and fly by night.
The moon hides me from peoples' sight.
Reach for me but always fail.
Trust in me when you set sail.

You can only see them at night. The light from the moon can make them hard to see, and it blocks our view of some of them. "Reach for the stars" is a saying for things that you can try to do but won't succeed at. Before the days of GPS, you used the position of the stars to see where your ship was.

Sometimes Inside

Sometimes inside,
Sometimes outside,
Sometimes it's not there at all.
Life needs form and structure,
Without me you would fall.

We have our skeletons inside, some insects and other creatures have them outside. Jellyfish and worms have no skeleton at all.

Hunter

The hunter far and wide will roam,
Like a ghost of sun and shadow.
First she'll brush then find the comb,
And then put on a dancing show.
Mother waits inside her home,
Where golden treasure flows.

*They fly away from the hive. Most of them are yellow and black.
They brush pollen on their legs and then return to the hive - the
honeycomb. Bees dance to tell the others where to find the
pollen. The queen bee stays at the hive where the honey is.*

Home

A home made out of water
A home as hard as steel
Where nighttime can be brilliant
And daytime darkness real.

*They're made of ice, that gets very hard in the cold. If you go
far enough north, in the summer the sun stays up long, but in
winter it's you hardly see it at all.*

Drowsy

Beneath the drowsy summer sun
I spread my golden hair.
From dawn until the day is done
I lie without a care.
My locks soon turn from gold to white,
As they get set to flee.
My hair comes loose and takes to flight
Adrift upon the breeze.

*They start off as yellow flowers. Then they turn white. Blown
away by the wind - or maybe by you!.*

Explanations

Downside

With downside dark
And upside pale
You run from me
When I turn tail.

*Most skunks have black fur on their stomach. And white fur
on their backs and tails. If they turn their tail up towards you,
they're getting ready to spray! Run away!*

Behind

One behind, and one between,
One stands on a hill.
Three on three, and three around,
A test of strength and skill.

*The catcher is "behind the plate" and the shortstop is between
second and third. The pitcher's on the mound (the hill). The
"three on three" are the basemen (first, second and third) and
the "three around" are the outfielders.*

Two Arms

Two arms, no hands
Four legs, no feet
One back, no spine
No lap, one seat.

*Many chairs have two arms and four legs, the chair back and
the seat.*

Two More Arms

Two short arms and head like a rock
Hanging around on a city block;
Wrench my arms, and you'll get wet,
But I'll get water from your pet.

*Picture what a fire hydrant looks like - it looks sort of like a little
guy with two arms. You'll find one on just about every city block.
Firemen open them up to get water. Dogs, on the other hand,
use them for something else.*

Ballet

I'm found in the ballet.
I'm a dance or a room.
I'm also hidden in
A helium balloon.
If you're having fun,
You might have one of me.
Hard and soft and basket,
Foot and base and tee.

Look for the letters, "ball" in many of the words. Or else put "ball" in front of or behind some of them to make a new word. At the end we're talking about hardball, softball, basketball, football, baseball and tee-ball.

Black and White

A killer clad in black and white.
Big, not sad, when blue.
Great and white inspired spite,
And gray's the other hue.

An orca (which is black and white) is called a "killer whale", even though it's actually a dolphin. Blue whales are the biggest animals on earth. Moby Dick was the Great White Whale. Gray whales are the other ones named for a color.

Sleeps

It sleeps for years and suddenly wakes
It shifts in bed, its body shakes.
Its blood flows red then turns to black.
It sleeps again but may come back.

When a volcano erupts there often isn't much warning. Lava flows red hot and then when it cools it turns black. Some volcanoes have been dormant for thousands of years, but who knows when they'll erupt again?

Explanations

Weather

In any weather we can thrive --
We flow across the plain,
And since we never are alive
We never can be slain.
Our presence you will never lack --
We never leave for long.
You chop us down -- we grow right back
An army thousands strong.

People and other furry animals live all over the place. When we say "plain", we actually mean skin or your head!

A Worker

A worker, tireless, straight and tall.
His own little room, he leans against the wall.
His dirty hair, hanging down,
Dry and dusty on the ground.
Push him around as much as you can,
Towards the edge, the edge of a pan.

Many people keep brooms in a "broom closet". Think of the bristles of the broom as his hair - dry, dusty and on the ground. When you're cleaning, you'll push him up to a dust pan.

Water and Sun

Born of the mixture of water and sun,
A marvel of beauty if ever was one.
A cloak of majesty worn by the sky,
No one can touch it but all dreamers try.

When sunlight passes through the water in the sky, we can see different colors. Have you ever tried to find the end of the rainbow?

Smiles

Always smiles or maybe frowns
Sinks in water, never drowns.
Catches prey on its barbed teeth
Hunts all day, but never eats.

Depending on how you hold the fishhook, it might look like a smile :) or a frown :(.

The Hidden Riddle - did you find it?

I'm never orange,
Though yellow can be.
A singer's friend,
In his songs you find me.
In a child's book kept,
And in poems too,
I'll bet you're surprised
Not to find me right here.

The word orange doesn't rhyme with any other word although yellow does. Songs usually have lots of rhymes in them. Did you notice how this riddle rhymed - until the very last line?

If you didn't find the hidden riddle, go back and look at all the pictures - do you see something interesting?

Explanations

Cloud Kingdom Games

Shadowman

Shadowman's Tricks and Traps contains a sampling of fiendishly clever puzzles to challenge either the individual adventurer, or a party of hearty treasure hunters.

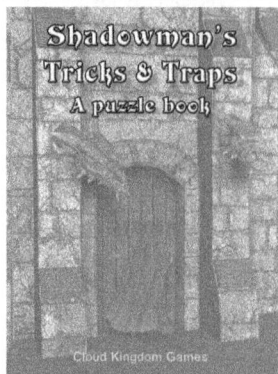

#50220 Shadowman's
          Twisted Treasury
#50222 Shadowman's Tricks & Traps

Shadowman's
Tricks & Traps
A puzzle book

Cloud Kingdom Games

Duality

Duality is an easy to learn, two-player card game. Each player works to build an unbroken path from one side to the other. They do this by replacing or adding cards connected to cards that are already played. Break your opponent's path while completing your own. Two players, ages 13+, about 15 minutes to play.

#50420 - Duality

duality

A two player strategic card game.

Ogre Bash

Ogre Bash is based on that time-honored Ogre tradition of standing around in a circle bashing each other on the head with clubs.

The Ogre Bash card game is just like that, except for the bashing each other on the head part. A humorous card game for three or more players, ages 13 and up.

#50401 Ogre Bash

Cloud Kingdom Games

Minions

Princess

Save her. Marry her. Sacrifice her. Devour her. Whatever.

7 Glory

In this light-hearted non-collectible card game, each player plays a Minor Deity and tries to get more Glory than the other Minor Deities in the neighborhood. Complete Quests like "*Kill the Orc and Take His Stuff*" or "*Avoid the Traps and Rob the Temple*" to get the Glory. Two or more players, ages ten and up.

Or for the Mutant Cowboy in all of us, there's also Minions: Cowboys & Aliens.

#50410 Minions: Darkness & Myth
#50411 Minions: Cowboys & Aliens

Building Dead Guys

Building Dead Guys card game pits two players against each other in a battle to the life. Each round a new Body Part is drawn. Both players bid secretly on it, the winner then places the Part onto their dead guy. Once you have a head, two arms and legs and a couple of organs, you win. Each Body part also has a one use ability which either helps you or hurts your opponent.

#50402 - Building Dead Guys

Need more Riddles?

Each Riddle Book is jam packed with Riddles from the RiddleMasters of Cloud Kingdom Games

#50302 Tower of the Riddle Master

#50303 Quest for the Riddle Stone

#50304 Riddle of the Unicorn

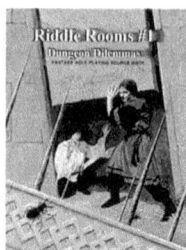

#50201 Riddle Rooms #1 - Dungeon Dilemmas

#50220 Shadowman's Twisted Treasury - a Collection of Killer Puzzles.

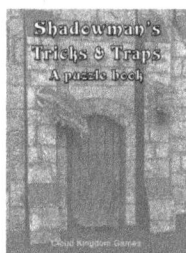

#50223 Shadowman's Tricks & Traps.

For more cool games, puzzles and riddles, or if you want to sign up for the FREE Riddle of the Week (check with your parents first) email, visit:

www.CloudKingdom.com

Cloud Kingdom Games

www.ingramcontent.com/pod-product-compliance
Lightning Source LLC
Chambersburg PA
CBHW060410050426
42449CB00009B/1947